500 YUCKY jokes!

PaRragon

Bath · New York · Singapore · Hong Kong · Cologne · Delhi · Melbourne

First published by Parragon in 2009

Parragon
Queen Street House
4 Queen Street
Bath BA1 1HE, UK

Copyright © Parragon Books Ltd 2009

ISBN 978-1-4075-7364-9

Printed in India

CONTENTS

SNOT, POO AND GUNKY GOO

Where does Dracula keep his valuables?

In a blood bank.

What do you get if you cross a Martian with a golf score?

A little green bogey .

Knock, knock.

Who's there?

Stan.

Stan who?

Stan back, I'm going to sneeze!

Knock, knock.

Who's there?

Pooh.

Pooh who?

Pooh, what an awful smell!

What did the tissue say
to the nose?
'Don't get snotty with me!'

What can you keep even if
you give it away?
A cold.

What is the difference between
bogeys and cabbage?
Kids don't eat cabbage.

What do you call a fairy with BO?
Stinkerbelle.

Why did the man have BO
on one side only?
He bought some Right Guard,
but couldn't find any Left Guard.

What did the nose say to the boy?
'Why are you always picking on me?'

Why was the nose so tired?
Because it had been running all day.

What is red and stupid?
A blood clot.

Why did the bogey cross the road?
Because he was tired
of getting picked on.

If a buttercup is yellow,
what colour is a hiccup?
Burple.

What makes snuffle rock music?
Electric catarrh.

What can you do if your
nose goes on strike?
Picket.

'Your brother's built upside down.'
'What do you mean?'
'His nose runs and his
feet smell.'

'What are you giving your little sister for Christmas?'

'I'm not sure. Last year I gave her chickenpox.'

'I was going to buy Grandad a handkerchief for Christmas but I didn't.'

'Why not?'

'I couldn't find one big enough for his nose!'

How can you stop your nose running?

Stick out your foot and trip it up.

What nut sounds like a sneeze?

A cashew.

What happened to the snake with a cold?

She adder viper nose.

What's brown and sounds like a bell?

Dung.

What's brown and sticky?

A stick.

What's thick and black and comes out of the ground and shouts 'Knickers!'?

Crude oil.

What is black, gushes out of the ground and shouts 'I beg your pardon'?

Refined oil.

What did the bath say to the toilet?

'You look a bit flushed.'

Mum: 'Stop picking your nose!'

Boy: 'Why? 'Snot fair!'

What happened when the nuclear scientist swallowed uranium?

He got atomic ache.

Which queen
had acne?
Mary Queen
of Spots.

How did the basketball
court get wet?
The players dribbled all over it.

What did one tonsil say to
the other?
'Get dressed; the doctor is
taking us out tonight.'

What's brown and steaming
and comes out of Cowes?
The Isle of Wight ferry.

What goes, 'Ha ha, plop!'?
Someone laughing their
head off.

What goes, 'Boo hoo, splat'?
Someone crying their eyes out.

'Doctor, doctor, there's
something wrong with
my stomach.'
'If you keep your coat
buttoned up no one will notice.'

How do you keep flies out
of the kitchen?
Coat the dining room in manure.

'Mummy, Mummy! Where have all your scabs gone?'
'Shut up and eat your cornflakes.'

What's green and hangs off trees?
Giraffe snot.

I have a green nose, three red mouths and four purple ears. What am I?
Ugly!

Why was the teacher cross-eyed?
She couldn't control her pupils.

What monster sits on the end of your finger?
The Bogeyman.

What's green and hangs off trees?
Giraffe snot.

What do you call someone who wipes their nose on their sleeve?
Green sleeves.

Why do golf players wear two pairs of underpants?
In case they get a hole in one.

What has four wheels and flies?
A rubbish truck.

When do cannibals cook their victims?
On Fry Day .

Knock, knock.
Who's there?
Kenny .
Kenny who?
Kenny you please open the door, I'm dying to go to the loo!

Ernie: 'My teacher was bitten by a dog yesterday .'
Bruce: 'How is she?'
Ernie: 'She's fine, but the dog died.'

What happens if you walk under a cow?

You might get a pat on the head.

What do you call Australian boxer shorts?

Down-underwear!

Why did the man put an eye in the freezer?

He wanted to make an icicle.

How do you get a tissue to dance?

Put a boogie in it!

How many farts does it take
to make a stinkbomb?
A phew!

Lifeguard: 'You're not
allowed to pee in the pool.'
Little Billy: 'But everyone
pees in the pool.'
Lifeguard: 'Maybe, but not
from the diving board.'

Why do gorillas have big fingers?
Because they have big nostrils!

How can you catch dandruff?
Shake your head over
a paper bag.

What's the difference between someone who's desperate for the lavatory and someone who's trapped in the lions' enclosure?
One is dying to go and the other is going to die.

Why shouldn't you swim on a full stomach?
It's much easier swimming in a full swimming pool.

Why did the boy laugh?
He hit his funny bone.

Where do you find giant snails?
On the ends of giants' fingers.

What do you call two burglars?
A pair of nickers.

A thief broke into the police station and stole all the toilets.
Police say they've got nothing to go on.

What do you call a Roman emperor with a cold?
Julius Sneezer.

What do you call a man with a bogey problem?
No one nose.

Why is Tigger always dirty?
Because he plays with Pooh.

What are you if you step into a cow pat?

An incowpoop.

Knock, knock.
Who's there?
Ahab.
Ahab who?
Ahab to go to the loo in a hurry!

What happens to cows in hot weather?

They give evaporated milk.

What's the highest place on earth you can go to the loo?

On the top of Mount Everest.

Why did the bee fly with his legs crossed?

To get to the BP station.

What is green and has four legs and two trunks?

Two seasick tourists.

Knock, knock.

Who's there?

Butter.

Butter who?

Butter be quick, I need to go to the loo.

What did the slug say as he slipped down the wall?

How slime flies!

How do you know your kitchen floor is dirty?

The slugs leave a trail on the floor that reads, 'Clean me'!

What do you get if you are hit on the head with an axe?

A splitting headache.

Why are teenage geese so shy?

Because they get goose pimples.

What's green and goes round and round at 60 miles an hour?

A frog in a liquidizer.

'Do you always wash in dirty water?'

'It wasn't dirty when I started.'

Where does Tarzan buy his underpants?

At a jungle sale.

Why did the toilet paper roll down the hill?

Because it wanted to get to the bottom.

What do you get if you cross a toad with a galaxy?

Star Warts.

What do you call an overweight ET?

An extra cholesterol.

Why does Wayne Rooney wear a bib?

Because he's always dribbling.

Why do bees have sticky hair?

They use honeycombs.

How can you tell which end of a worm is the head?

Tickle its middle and see which end smiles.

What do you call a snowman in the Sahara?

A puddle.

What's yellow and very dangerous?

Shark-infested custard.

What has two legs, a broom and flies?

A caretaker covered in jam.

Why did the boy bury his dad in the snow?

Because he wanted frozen pop!

What do you get if you cross a snake with a pie?

A pie-thon.

Mum: 'Fred, you've been fighting again. You've lost your front teeth!'

Fred: 'No I haven't, Mum. They're in my pocket.'

What's the difference between a musician and a dead body?

One composes while the other decomposes.

What happened to the robber who fell into a cement mixer?

He became a hardened criminal.

If H2O is on the inside
of a fire hydrant, what
is on the outside?
K9P.

What do worms leave around
their bath?
Scum of the earth.

'Do you know the way
to Bath?'
'I always use soap and water.'

What did the musician say
to the audience?
Ear we go again.

'I just swallowed a bone!'
'Are you choking?'
'No, I'm serious.'

Why did granny put her hands to her mouth when she sneezed?

To catch her teeth.

Mum: 'Did you know that most accidents happen in the kitchen?'

Scott: 'Yes, I have to eat them'!

Why was the sand wet?

Because the sea weed.

What's green with red spots?

A frog with chicken pox.

How did the elf get indigestion?

He kept gobblin' his dinner.

ZOMBIES, GHOSTS AND MINGING MONSTERS

What kind of monster loves to dance?

A boogieman.

How do monsters like their eggs?

Terri-fried.

Why wouldn't the ghost cross the road?

He had no guts.

What is a monster's favourite ballet?

Swamp Lake.

The Vampire's Victim by E. Drew Blood.

What only goes out at night and goes chomp, suck... 'Ouch!'
A vampire with a rotten fang.

What did the mother vampire say to her son?
'Hurry up and eat your breakfast before it clots.'

What's a ghoul's favourite breakfast cereal?
Rice creepies.

Why did the vampire's lunch give her heartburn?
It was a stake sandwich.

Why did the vampire need mouthwash?

She had bat breath.

What does a vampire take for a bad cold?

Coffin drops.

Which creature is the most likely to have indigestion?

A goblin.

When does a skeleton laugh?

When something tickles his funny bone.

Why is it so easy to fool vampires?

Because they're suckers.

Which instrument does a skeleton play?

A trombone.

How did the kid catch Egyptian flu?

He caught it from his mummy.

First monster: 'That girl just rolled her eyes at me.'

Second monster: 'Don't you think you'd better roll them back?'

What do you get when you cross a monster's brain with an elastic band?

A real stretch of the imagination.

What did one skeleton prisoner say to the other skeleton prisoner?

'If we had the guts, we'd get out of here!'

What does Dracula say when he meets someone new?

'Hello, I'm very pleased to eat you!'

Why did the vampire go to jail?

Because he robbed the blood bank.

Why don't skeletons
go to discos?
They have no body to
dance with.

What's a baby zombie's
favourite toy?
A deadly bear.

Where do ghosts like to swim?
In the Dead Sea.

Did you hear about the
zombie who went on
a cruise ship?
In the restaurant he
refused the menu and
asked for the passenger list.

What did the zombie write at Christmas?

His chopping list.

What is as sharp as a vampire's fang?

His other fang.

Why didn't the skeleton go bungee-jumping?

He didn't have the guts.

What is a vampire's favourite kind of coffee?

De-coffin-ated!

What do vampires read to their children at night?

Bite-time stories.

Why did the skeleton cross
the road?

Because it wanted to go to the
Body Shop.

Why do scary monsters have
so many ears?

To make them more eerie.

What would you call the ghost
of a door-to-door salesman?

A dead ringer.

Why is Frankenstein such
good fun?

Because he'll have you
in stitches.

What do you say to a monster with two heads?

'Hello, and hello to you, too.'

What's a monster's favourite game?

Swallow the leader.

What do you call a fat vampire?

Fatula.

What kind of music do mummies listen to?

Wrap.

Why do vampires have chickpeas, lentils and beans with their meals?

Because they'll eat anything with pulses.

Why did the vampire keep brushing her hair?

She came from Transyl-vain-ia.

Why did the festering zombie stay in bed?

He felt rotten.

What do you call an undead cow?

Zombeef.

Where do zombies eat lunch?
At the cadaver-teria.

How can you tell when a vampire
has been in a bakery?
All the jam has been sucked out
of the jam doughnuts.

How can you help a
starving cannibal?
Give them a hand!

What did the cannibal say when
he came home and found his wife
chopping up a python and
a pygmy?
'Oh no, not snake and pygmy
pie again!'

Why did the monster
go into hospital?
To have his
ghoul-stones removed.

What should you do if you go
on a picnic with King Kong?
Give him the biggest bananas.

Why don't cannibals eat
weatherforecasters?
Because they give them wind!

What do cannibals eat at
picnics?
Hard-boiled legs.

What happened to the magician who did a show for cannibals?

He went down really well.

Why did the vampire become an artist?

Because he was so good at drawing blood.

What do you get if you cross a skeleton with a cowboy?

The Bone Ranger.

What happened at the cannibals' wedding?

They toasted the bride and groom.

What is a vampire's favourite type of boat?

Blood vessels.

What's a monster's favourite food?

Ghoul-ash.

What is Dracula's favourite ice cream?

Vein-illa.

What's a ghost's favourite desert?

I scream.

Why are mummies the most selfish monsters?

Because they are all wrapped up in themselves.

Boy cannibal: 'I hate my baby sister.'

Mum cannibal: 'Well leave her to one side and just eat your chips.'

Boy cannibal: 'Mum, can I bring my friend over for tea?'
Mum cannibal: 'Of course, dear, put him in the fridge and we'll have him later.'

Why do ghosts always hang around in threes?
Because two's company, three's a shroud.

What do you call a corpse with nothing to do?
Bored stiff.

What do you get if you cross an ugly witch with a clown?
A frightful brew-ha-ha.

Knock, knock.

Who's there?

Donna.

Donna who?

Donna look now but there's a great big monster right behind you!

What's green, very tall and mopes in the corner?

The incredible sulk.

What do you get if you cross a witch's cat with a lemon?

A sour puss.

What do sea monsters like
to eat?
Fish and ships.

What do cannibals eat
for pudding?
Chocolate-covered aunts.

Why was the zombie so grumpy?
She woke up too early in
the mourning.

What's the difference between
a deadly disease and a Klingon?
One's smallpox and the other
mauls Spock.

Knock, knock.

Who's there?

Dracula.

Dracula who?

Dracula drink in one go!

What do monsters sing
at Christmas?

'Deck the Halls with Poison Ivy'.

Who won the monsters'
beauty contest?

No body!

What did the boy vampire say
to the glamorous girl vampire?

'Hello, gore-juice.'

What do you call a skeleton
who's a friend?

A bony crony.

What happened to the zombie after he ate the comedian?

He got a funny feeling in his stomach.

What kind of beans do zombies like to eat?

Human beans!

How does a zombie greet a human being?

'Pleased to eat you.'

What did the zombie say to his zombie friend?

'Excuse me, is this your finger?'

Why couldn't the witch give
a speech?
She had a frog in her throat.

What did the skeleton
weatherforecaster say?
Tomorrow's weather will be
bone dry...

What kind of plate does
a skeleton eat his dinner on?
A bone china plate.

Why did the skeleton go
to the party?
To have a rattling good time.

How does an undertaker start a letter?
Tomb it may concern.

How do undertakers speak?
Gravely.

What do ghosts like for breakfast?
Dreaded Wheat.

What do Italian ghosts like for supper?
Spook-hetti.

What are twin vampires called?
Blood Brothers.

How does a monster count up to 30?
On its fingers.

What day of the week do monsters eat people?
Chewsday.

Why do monsters forget what you tell them?
Because it goes in one ear and out of all the others.

What did Frankenstein's monster say when he was struck by lightning?
'I needed that.'

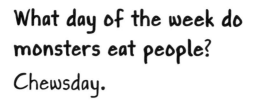

How did Frankenstein's monster eat his food?

He bolted it down.

Why was Dracula sad?

His love was in vein.

What do monsters have on their toast?

Scream cheese.

Where do Martians get their eggs?

From the little green hen.

What's a vampire's favourite feast?

Fangs-giving Day dinner.

What kind of dog does Dracula have?

A bloodhound.

How do you make a witch itch?

Take away her 'w'.

What did the skeleton say while riding his motorbike?

'I'm bone to be wild!'

Why didn't the skeleton enjoy work?

His heart wasn't in it.

MAGGOTS, MOULD AND FOUL FOOD

What is a vampire's favourite type of fruit?

A neck-trine.

What's a goblin's favourite flavour drink?

Lemon 'n' slime.

What do skeletons say before they eat?

'Bone appetit!'

'Why won't you take your sister with you when you go fishing?'

'She eats all my maggots.'

Who wrote 'Living on Garlic and Onions'?

I. Malone.

Why are eggs losers?
Because they're always beaten.

Which British town is known for its bad meat?
Oldham.

What's worse than biting into an apple and finding a maggot?
Biting into an apple and finding half a maggot!

Why did the skeleton go to the Chinese takeaway?
To get some spare ribs.

What's yellow, red and white
and flies at 500 miles per hour?
A pilot's egg-and-tomato sandwich.

I eat my peas with honey . I've
done it all my life. It makes the
peas taste funny, but it keeps
them on the knife!

'I'd like an elephant
sandwich, please.'
'I'm sorry, we don't do
elephant sandwiches.'
'Why not?'
'We haven't any bread.'

'If you eat any more you'll burst!'

'Then you'd better watch out, because I'm going to have some pudding!'

What do vampires like for breakfast?

Ready Neck.

What's a vampire's favourite fruit?

A blood orange.

How can you join Dracula's fan club?

Send your name, address and blood group.

Why did the skeleton feel the cold so badly?

The wind blew straight through him.

What does a vampire have at 11 o'clock every morning?

A coffin break.

Why don't vampires get fat?

They eat necks to nothing.

What did the monster say to its victim?

'So long, it's been good to gnaw you.'

What do you call a monster with three eyes and four mouths?

Very ugly!

How do you greet a three-headed monster?

'Hello, hello, hello.'

What do ghosts eat with roast beef?

Grave-y .

What did the sea monster say when it saw a submarine?

'Oh, good, tinned food.'

What do country monsters like to eat?

Shepherd's pie, made with real shepherds.

What do monsters eat with bread and cheese?

Pickled organs.

What do baby monsters say at bedtime?

'Read me a gory .'

How do you tell when a corpse is angry?

It flips its lid.

Why were the skeleton's teeth chattering?

He was chilled to the bone.

What's a monster's favourite football team?

Slitherpool.

What do zombies like for lunch?

Baked beings on toast.

What fish is good for pudding?

A jellyfish.

'Waiter! What kind of soup is this?'

'It's bean soup, sir.'

'I don't care what it's been, what is it now?'

What do you get if you cross a pig with a zebra?

Striped sausages.

If an apple a day keeps the doctor away, what does an onion a day do?

It keeps everyone away!

Did you hear the story of the three eggs?

Too bad.

Knock, knock.
Who's there?
Ooze.
Ooze who?
Ooze eaten all the toffees?

'Waiter! There's a button
in my salad!'
'Yes, sir, it's off the jacket potato.'

'Waiter! This coffee tastes
like mud!'
'I'm not surprised, sir, it was
ground just a few minutes ago.'

What's white on the outside,
green on the inside, and hops?
A frog sandwich.

What's the difference between a lavatory brush and a chocolate biscuit? You can't dip a lavatory brush in your tea.

What's the difference between tapioca pudding and frogspawn? Not a lot!

'Is that steak pie I smell?'
'It is, and you do.'

'You had egg for breakfast, I can see it on your chin.'
'No I didn't, that was yesterday.'

'Waiter! There's a worm on my plate!'
'That's not a worm, sir, that's your sausage.'

What happens if you play table tennis with a bad egg? First it goes ping, then it goes pong.

What kind of sandwich speaks for itself? A tongue sandwich.

'Waiter, there's a fly in my soup.' 'Don't worry, sir. It wiped its feet on the bread roll.'

'Waiter, why have you got your thumb on my apple pie?' 'To stop it falling on the floor again, madam.'

'Waiter, this fish smells terrible.'

'Yes, it's a case of long time, no sea.'

Where's the best place to have the school sickroom?

Next to the canteen!

'Waiter! This egg is bad!'

'Don't blame me, sir, I only laid the table!'

'Waiter! What is that fly doing on my ice cream?'

'Learning to ski, sir.'

Should you eat sausages with your fingers?

No, fingers should be eaten separately .

What do you get if you cross a birthday cake with a tin of baked beans?

A cake that blows out its own candles.

'What are you going to do with that horse manure?'

'Put it on my strawberries.'

'Really? We put cream on ours!'

'Is this cloudy lemonade?'

'No, it's just the glass that's dirty.'

What's a two-handed cheese?

One that you eat with one hand while you hold your nose with the other.

'Waiter! What's this in my soup?'
'I don't know, I can't tell one
insect from another.'

What do frogs like to drink?
Croaka Cola.

'Waiter, there's a dead fly in
my soup!'
'I'm afraid they can't swim, sir.'

'Waiter! This food's not fit
for a pig!'
'I'll bring you some that is, sir.'

'Waiter, there's a film on
my soup!'
'Have you seen it before, sir?'

'I don't like all the flies in this restaurant.'

'Tell me which ones you particularly dislike and I'll have them thrown out.'

What's a mushroom?
A place where school dinners are prepared.

What's a skeleton's favourite barbecue?
Spare ribs.

Why did the bacon groan?
Because the egg's yolks were so bad.

What's a nuclear scientist's favourite food?
Fission chips.

What's does a dustbin man have for lunch?
Junk food.

What do you get if you cross a pig with a naked person?
Streaky bacon.

Three convicts were in court for escaping from prison.
The judge said: 'I would like to know two things. First, why did you escape?'
One of the three men stepped forward. 'Your honour, we escaped because the food is so awful.'
'I see. And second, what did you use to smash open the bars of your cell?'
The prisoner replied, 'The toast, your honour.'

Did you hear about the man who fell into a vat of curry?

He slipped into a korma.

What's short, green and goes camping?

A boy sprout.

Mum: 'Eat your spinach, it'll put colour in your cheeks.'

Mickey: 'But I don't want green cheeks!'

'Waiter, this soup tastes funny .'
'Then why aren't you laughing?'

What do you get if you cross
a Scottish legend and a bad egg?
The Loch Ness pongster.

'Waiter! My souffle's flat.'
'That's because I sat on it, sir.'

What does a termite eat
for breakfast?
Oak-meal.

What weighs two tonnes and
sticks to the roof of
your mouth?
Peanut butter and rhino sandwiches.

What's white on the outside, green on the inside and comes with relish and onions?

A hot frog.

What happens if you give your mouse some smelly cheese?

You make an awful mess of your computer.

Teacher: 'Is eating chicken good for your health?'

Dan: 'Not if you're a chicken.'

What did the maggot say to his friend when he got stuck in an apple?

'Worm your way out of that one!'

What's yellow, wiggly and dangerous?

A maggot with a bad attitude.

Why do worms taste like chewing gum?

Because they're Wrigley's.

'Waiter, waiter! Why is my steak pie all smashed up?'

'Well, you did ask me to step on it, sir.'

Have you heard the one about the giant fruit cake?

It's very hard to swallow.

What's brown, hairy and sneezes?
A coconut with a cold.

What happened to the
butcher who was late
for work?
He got the chop.

What's a fishmonger's
favourite film?
The Codfather.

How do they serve burgers in
Transylvania?
Very rare-ly.

What's the best time of year to see a man-eating tiger? I don't know — but at Christmas, it's easy to see a man eating turkey.

What do you get if you cross a cat with a parrot? A carrot.

Where do tough chickens come from? Hard-boiled eggs.

'Why have you got a sausage behind your ear?' 'Oh dear, I must have eaten my pencil for lunch.'

What is an elf's favourite
kind of birthday cake?
Shortcake.

What happened when the chef
found a daddy-long-legs
in the salad?
It became a daddy-short-legs.

What vegetable should you
never have on a boat?
A leek.

Why are cooks cruel?
Because they beat eggs, whip
cream and batter fish.

What do golfers eat for lunch?
Club sandwiches.

What happened to the man who stole an apple pie?
He was taken into custard-y .

Why did the grape go out with a prune?
Because he couldn't get a date.

Nat: 'Gran, why have you got custard in one ear and jelly in the other?'
Gran: 'Speak up dear. I'm a trifle deaf.'

BEASTS, FLEAS AND FURRY FRIENDS

What do you get when you cross a scary werewolf with a sculptor?

Hairy Potter.

What's soft, mouldy and flies?

A spoiled bat.

Why couldn't the young skunk have a chemistry set for Christmas?

His mother said it would stink the house out.

Why did the skunk take an aspirin?

Because it had a stinking cold.

Why are skunks always fighting?
They enjoy raising a stink.

Did you hear about the dog that lived on garlic?
Its bark was worse than its bite.

How can you find out where a flea has bitten you?
You start from scratch.

Why do giraffes have such long necks?
Because their feet smell.

How do you start a flea race?

'One, two, flea — go!'

How can you tell if an elephant's been in your fridge?

By the footprints in the butter.

What's the best way to prevent the rash you get from biting fleas?

Stop biting fleas!

What did the police officer say when a black widow spider ran down his back?

'You're under a vest!'

Why did the cat stop talking?
There was a paws in the conversation.

What do you call a dog with a cold?
A choo-wawa.

What has four legs and flies?
A dead sheep.

What do you get if you cross a bear with a skunk?
Winnie the Pooh.

What's the difference between a dog and a flea?
A dog can have fleas, but a flea can't have dogs.

What do you get if you cross a cow with a camel?
Lumpy milkshakes.

What do you give a seasick elephant?
Lots of room!

'Tom gave me his pig.'
'You can't keep it here. What about the smell?'
'The pig won't mind.'

'What kind of bird impressions do you do?'
'I eat worms.'

What do you give a pony that has a cold?

Cough stirrup.

How much did the fish weigh?

It was off the scales.

How do you stop a skunk from smelling?

Cut off its nose.

'Help! A shark's just bitten off my foot!'

'Which one?'

'How should I know? All sharks look the same to me.'

'My friend said you weren't
fit to live with pigs.'
'And what did you say?'
'Oh, I stuck up for you.
I said of course you were
fit to live with pigs.'

What do you give a pig with a rash?
Ointment.

What do you get if you cross a
seagull with a parrot?
A bird that poos on your head and
then says, 'Sorry .'

What do you get if you cross
a skunk with a boomerang?
A bad smell you can't get rid of.

What do you get if you cross a skunk with a wasp?

Something that stinks and stings.

What's worse than a giraffe with a stiff neck?

An elephant with a cold.

'Keep that dog out of the house, it's full of fleas.'

'Rover, don't go in the house. It's full of fleas.'

What happens when a flea is very angry?

It gets hopping mad.

What do you get if you cross an alligator with a tummy bug?

An illigator.

Why wouldn't the snake go on the weighing machine?

Because he had his own scales.

What's the most contagious disease in China?

Kung flu.

Mum: 'Why did you put a mouse in Auntie's bed?'

George: 'Because I couldn't find a spider.'

What's a flea's favourite
TV show?
Scratch of the day .

What do you get if you cross
a skunk with an owl?
A bird that smells but
doesn't give a hoot!

Customer: 'Do you have
a sheep's head?'
Butcher: 'No, it's just my funny
haircut.'

How did the scorpion story end?
There was a sting in the tale.

What do you do with a sick horse?
Take it to horspital.

What can fly underwater?
A bluebottle in a submarine.

Two fleas were on their way into town.
'Shall we walk?' asked one.
'No,' said the second. 'Let's take a dog.'

How did the two fleas travel from London to Edinburgh?
By itch-hiking.

Did you hear what happened to the flea circus?

A dog came along and stole the show!

Why did the woolly mammoth eat the stupid man?

Because someone said he was nuts.

What do you call an exploding monkey?

A ba-boom!

Why do cows lie down close together?

To keep each udder warm.

What did the mouse say when it broke its front teeth?

'Hard cheese.'

What do you get if you cross a chicken with a cement mixer?

A bricklayer.

What would happen if tarantulas were as big as horses?

If one bit you, you could ride it to hospital!

What is a flea's favourite book?

'The Itch-hiker's Guide to the Galaxy!'

Did you hear about the skunk that was shot into space?
It stunk to high heaven.

What films do vultures love?
Carrion films.

What do you get if you cross a dog with a skunk?
Rid of the dog.

What's the difference between a wolf and a flea?
One howls on the prairie and the other prowls on the hairy.

What do you call a camel with no humps?

Humphrey.

Why did the hedgehog cross the road?

To see his flatmate.

What do elephants wear under their trousers?

Ele-pants.

Why are elephants tall, grey and wrinkly?
Because if they were small, white and smooth, they would be aspirins.

What's big and grey and puts everyone into a trance?
A hypno-potamus.

What do you get if you cross a polar bear with a flower?
I don't know , but I'm not going to smell it.

What's big and grey and has trouble with personal hygiene?
A smellephant.

Which side of a cat has
the most fur?

The outside.

Why did the cow cross
the road?

To get to the udder side.

What lies on the ground a
thousand feet up and smells?

A dead millipede.

What did the boy centipede
say to the girl centipede?

'May I hold your hand,
hand, hand...'

How can you identify a baby snake?
By its rattle.

Why did the chicken footballer
get sent off?
For fowl language.

'Your dog's really lazy'
'Why do you say that?'
'Yesterday I watered the
garden and he never lifted
a leg to help me.'

Knock, knock.
Who's there?
Thumping.
Thumping who?
**Thumping with lots of
legs just crawled up
your trousers.**

**Where do you find a dog with
no legs?**
Right where you left him!

**What do birds give out
on Halloween?**
Tweets.

Why do rabbits eat rust?
Because it's a type of car rot.

What's a slug?
A snail with a housing problem.

Charlie: 'I was arrested for stealing a pig.'
Ben: 'How did they catch you?'
Charlie: 'The pig squealed.'

How does an octopus go to war?
Fully-armed.

What says, 'Quick, quick'?
A duck with hiccups.

What goes 99-thump,
99-thump, 99-thump?
A centipede with a
wooden leg.

What do you call a
greasy chicken?
A slick chick.

Why did the chewing gum
cross the road?
Because it was stuck to the
chicken's foot.

What do you get if you cross a bear with an old pair of socks?
Winnie the Pooh.

'Waiter! Do you have frogs' legs?'
'No, sir, it's just the way I walk.'

Why did the chicken footballer get a yellow card?
He committed a fowl.

How can you stop fish
from smelling?
Cut off their noses.

What does a triceratops sit on?
Its tricera-bottom.

'It's raining cats and dogs!'
'I know, I just stepped in
a poodle.'

What did the frog order
at McDonald's?
French flies and
a Diet Croak.

What do you get when you cross a pig with a centipede?
Bacon and legs.

What's the difference between a teenager and a leopard?
One's covered in spots and sleeps all day and the other is a leopard.

What looks like half a cat?
The other half.

REPULSIVE AND REVOLTING RANDOM JOKES

Why are cemeteries
noisy places?

Because of the coffin.

What skeleton was once
the Emperor of France?

Napoleon Bone-apart.

What is round, white and
smells awful?

A ping-pong ball.

'Your socks have got
holes in them!'

'How else would I get my
feet in?'

'Is your bad tooth better now?'
'I don't know, I left it
with the dentist."

'She has a heart of gold.'
'It must match her teeth.'

Why did Henry VIII have
so many wives?
He liked to chop and change.

What is the smelliest city
in America?
Phew York.

How can you stop a cold in the head going to your chest?
Tie a knot in your neck!

Which country has no fat people?
Finland.

Hypnotist: 'When I count to three, you will no longer be shy and you will be able to speak your mind. 1-2-3...'
Patient: 'Thanks for your help, fatso.'

What happens when Prince William burps?
He gets a royal pardon.

Where did the broken action man go to get fixed?

To the plastic surgeon.

How many ears does Captain Kirk have?

Three. A left ear, a right ear and a Final Frontier.

Why isn't your nose 12 inches long?

Because then it would be a foot.

What do you get if you cross a snake and a pig?

A boar constrictor.

What did the police officer say to his belly button?

You're under a vest.

Dentist: 'Have your teeth ever been checked?'

Tom: 'No, they've always been white.'

What is a mosquito's favourite sport?

Skin-diving!

Where can you see a really ugly monster?

In the mirror!

'How did Mum know you hadn't washed?'

'I forgot to wet the towel.'

Why did the mummy stay in the doctor's surgery for five hours?

He was getting himself bandaged up.

What did the vampire say to the doctor?

'Doctor, I can't stop coffin.'

'Doctor, I think I've been bitten by a vampire.'

'Drink this glass of water.'

'Will it make me better?'

'No, but I'll be able to see if your neck leaks.'

What do you get if
Batman and Robin are
run over by a steamroller?
Flagman and Ribbon.

What do hangmen read?
Noosepapers.

'Doctor, doctor, I'm at
death's door!'
'Don't worry, I'll pull you through.'

'Doctor, doctor, I'm having
trouble breathing!'
'Don't worry, I'll soon
put a stop to that!'

'Doctor, doctor, my little boy has just swallowed a bullet!'

'Well, don't point him at me!'

'What's frozen water?'

'Ice water.'

'And what's frozen tea?'

'Iced tea.'

'And what's frozen ink?'

'Iced ink.'

'I know you do!'

'I like your Easter tie.'

'Why do you call it my Easter tie?'

'Because it's covered in egg.'

'Doctor, doctor, I keep thinking I'm a dustbin!'

'Don't talk rubbish.'

Why did the fish blush?

Because it saw the ship's bottom.

Did you hear about the boy scout whose beret blew off in a field full of cows?

He had to try on 20 before he found it!

What's an ig?

An eskimo's house without a loo.

Knock, knock.
Who's there?
Sonia.
Sonia who?
Sonia shoe, I can smell it from here.

What do you call a woman with two lavatories on her head?
Lulu.

What do you call little white things in your head that bite?
Teeth.

Why are monsters so clever?
Because two heads are better than one.

'Did you hear the joke about the dirty T-shirt?'

'No.'

'That's one on you!'

'That film gave me a cold, slithery feeling down my neck.'

'So that's where my ice cream went!'

'Do you know anyone who's been on the telly?'

'My little brother did once but he can use a potty now.'

What did one eye say to the other?

'Between you and me something smells.'

'Does your mum cook by gas or electricity?'
'I don't know, I've never tried to cook her.'

'Did you hear the story about the dustbin lorry?'
'Yes, it was a load of old rubbish.'

Why can't a steam engine sit down?
Because it has a tender behind.

Why do snowmen make good soldiers?
They keep a cool head under pressure.

What has a bottom at
the top?
A leg.

Have you heard the joke about
the dirty window?
You wouldn't see through it!

What do you get if you
pull your knickers up
to your armpits?
A chest of drawers.

What's the best cure for
water on the knee?
Drainpipe trousers.

What do you call a man who
was born in Scotland, lived in
Wales, and died in England?
Dead.

Why do snowmen have to go to the doctor a lot?

They're always catching colds.

A man who works in a butcher's shop is 6 feet tall, has a 38' waist and wears size 11 shoes. What does he weigh?

Meat.

What do you call an exploding general?

Napoleon Blownapart.

What happened to the depressed dustbin man?

He was down in the dumps.

Where did the skeleton king hold court?

In the bone room.

What did the slug say as he slipped down the wall?

'How slime flies!'

Where does a burger bar owner go on holiday?

Greece.

Knock, knock.

Who's there?

Nick.

Nick who?

Nick R. Elastic.

What do you get when you cross a chicken with a ghost?

A poultry-geist.

What's a witch's favourite dessert?

Black pudding.

'Waiter! Was that cottage pie?'

'Yes, sir.'

'Well, fetch a doctor. I think I've just swallowed a window!'

What did the kebab say as it was about to be put on the skewer?

'Spear me, spear me!'

What shoes do you make from banana skins?

Slippers.

Did you hear about the man who crossed the Alps twice without taking a bath?

The dirty double-crosser!

What are the strongest vegetables in the world?

Muscle sprouts.

Why did the burglar cut off the legs of his bed?

He wanted to lie low.

Why are sausages bad mannered?

Because they spit in the frying pan.

What was green and used
to hold up stagecoaches?
Dick Gherkin.

What do you get when you
cross a chicken with a ghost?
A poultry-geist.

'My dad has hundreds of
people under him.'
'Really? What does he do?'
'He cuts the grass in
the cemetery .'

Why did the bald man stick his
head out of the window?
To get some fresh air.

What happened when someone hit the skeleton on his shins?

He hadn't a leg to stand on.

'Doctor, Doctor! I think I've swallowed a ten-pound note.'

'Come back tomorrow and we'll see if there's any change.'

What happened to the woman the magician sawed in half?

She's now living in London and Glasgow.

Why are monsters and mums similar?

They both have eyes in the backs of their heads.

What is red and dangerous?

Strawberry and tarantula jelly

Why did Archie's gran knit him three socks?

Because he told her he had grown another foot.

Who has the biggest boots in the British Army?

The soldier with the biggest feet!

How do you make antifreeze?

Hide her nightie!

Why did the traffic light turn red?

You would too if you had to change in the middle of the street.

What was purple and conquered the world?
Alexander the Grape.

What did the guillotine operator say to his wife?
'I'm just off to do a bit of chopping.'

Old lady: 'Can I try that dress on in the window?'
Shop assistant: 'No, you'll have to use the changing room!'

Customer: 'Is this the second-hand shop?'
Shopkeeper: 'Yes, that's right.'
Customer: 'Good — I'll have one for my watch then, please.'

Man: Officer, what is the quickest way to get to hospital?
Police officer: 'Lie down in the middle of the road, sir.'

A lorry load of wigs was stolen last night.
Police are combing the area.

Two brothers have been arrested: one for stealing batteries and swallowing them, and the other for stealing fireworks. One has been charged and the other was let off.

Why did the rubber chicken cross the road?
To stretch her legs.